A Place Where Clouds Are Flowing

poems by

Han-Jae Lee

Finishing Line Press
Georgetown, Kentucky

A Place Where Clouds Are Flowing

Copyright © 2017 by Han-Jae Lee
ISBN 978-1-63534-339-7 First Edition
All rights reserved under International and Pan-American Copyright Conventions.
No part of this book may be reproduced in any manner whatsoever without written permission from the publisher, except in the case of brief quotations embodied in critical articles and reviews.

ACKNOWLEDGMENTS

I would like to thank the following journals for their publication of individual poems in previous versions:

"Cobweb" ~ *The Catamaran Literary Reader*
"Flower Watch" ~ *The Monterey Poetry Review*
"The Sorrow" ~ *The Monterey Poetry Review*
"Invisible Leash" ~ *CAESURA*
"Vine Rose" ~ *Literary Movement & Trend*
"While Polishing Darkness" ~ *Literature World*
"Greens' Rebellion" ~ *Vision of Poetry*

Many thanks to the publisher and editors at Finishing Line Press for selecting this chapbook for publication and for being so nice.
Special thanks to beloved my family and friends who gave me support and encouragement during the writing of this book
And gratitude to all of my teachers and poets who helped me to shape these poems: Alexander E. Braun, Barbara Beswetherick, Judy Bernstein, Yvonne Cannon, Magdalena Montagne, Jennifer Franklin, Gillian Cumming, Kenneth Share, Aubrey Moncrieffe, Rosanne English, Gi-Taek Kim, Su-Ik Lee.

Publisher: Leah Maines
Editor: Christen Kincaid
Cover Art: Mike Seungwook Lee
Author Photo: Mike Seungwook Lee
Cover Design: Elizabeth Maines McCleavy

Printed in the USA on acid-free paper.
Order online: www.finishinglinepress.com
also available on amazon.com

Author inquiries and mail orders:
Finishing Line Press
P. O. Box 1626
Georgetown, Kentucky 40324
U. S. A.

Table of Contents

Invisible Leash	1
Another World	2
Cobweb	3
Fireflies in the Backyard	4
Lilacs Bloom Again	5
Magnolia	6
Vine Rose	7
Apple Memories	8
April	9
Weeds' Rebellion	10
Journey with No Definite Objective	11
Story of the Half Moon	12
A Writing Class by the Railroad	13
A Place Where Clouds Are Flowing	14
In a Blacksmith Shop	15
Summer High Noon	16
Cigarette Butts	17
At the Margaret Mitchell House in Atlanta	18
At a Shopping Mall	19
Korea My Homeland	20
Flower Watch	21
The Sorrow	22
Faded Letter	23
A Lucky Day	24
Pedestrian Crosswalk at Times Square	25
The Observation Deck of the Empire State Building	26
Times Square	27
While Polishing Darkness	28
The Snail	29
White Porcelain Vase	30

Invisible Leash

At the training center a dog is tied to a stake—
a taut leash restrains him.

All day long he keeps trying to go further away
as if there were some chance of escape.

Sometimes he seems to forget his shackles.
And suddenly he rushes forward quickly.

But each time the leash tightens even more
and his body is jerked into the air.

Although he struggles with every fiber of his being
the distance he can move is not increased or decreased, and he seems diminished.

Today, the dog's trainer unties his leash.
At first the dog refuses to run forward—but leaps furiously in place.

Then even after he goes out a sizable distance he returns.
There is no leash now, but the distance between dog and stake is still taut.

Another World

I talked about the past with people I did not know
who looked like they came from dreams.

Their faces seemed picturesque
like the surface of meandering streams.
Their voices were a gentle breeze.

We walked along the village road—
the wildflowers in full bloom,
downy clouds dotting the sky.

Then, like an illusion
these strangers passed through the flowers
one by one.

I stopped walking and took a closer look at the flowers
comprised entirely of diverse unknowns.
Each one having its own life and universe.

After all the people were gone
I could only see myself.
A man who stood behind me.

Cobweb

A spider, all alone, is building a cobweb in the corner of the hamlet.
His house waves in the breeze, shaded by a drift of clouds.

Though it is only sounds and sunshine that he hauls up,
he mends the net strand by strand, as if according to musical notation.

Which line has to be installed first or last? How long?
He is a skilled carpenter, humming to himself as he builds.

"What stays where the winds have passed?"
"How long will I have to wait?

Though it is only a shadow in the moonlight and on the morning dew,
he is never giving up on his house.

He continues to inhabit the garden
where the sparrows twitter and the children chatter.

The spider is conceiving a dream of a loving nest
within the cosmos that hugs the sky, villages and byways.

Fireflies in the Backyard

In the soft summer New Jersey night
fireflies in my backyard
flitting here and there
illuminating the blackness.

Each summer the fireflies return
reminding me of my childhood in Korea
in the rural community
where we were too poor to buy light.

Sometimes too poor to own a candle,
we collected fireflies in a basket
and read books by their sparks.

Fireflies delightedly giving off their radiance
brightening the dark garden.

Lilacs Bloom Again

Lilacs bloom again.
Lilacs bloom again.
Light purple lilacs bloom again
by the grave of my lover.

Spring has come again.
Spring breezes have blown in again.

Once I thought that the memory of our first kiss
under the lilac bush in the evening
and the solemn vow
like golden flowers
would vanish like a breeze
and be gone completely.

I made every effort to erase these memories, but in vain.
Now lilacs awaken within me the forgotten faint fragrance
and her warm breath.
Her bright smile
revealed by the lilac.

At first I hated these lilacs.
Forgotten lover,
Unforgettable lover.
She comes with the lilacs and vanishes silently.

Alas! I would never send her away.
And I call her name repeatedly.
Only my sorrow and sighing echoes into air.
Lilacs bloom again.

Magnolia

Just when I am getting into my car
someone seems to call to me.
I look back hastily.

I see my mother wearing white clothes
and smiling brightly beyond the gate of the cemetery.

I return to her
as she waves both hands emphatically and says to me:

*"Oh no, no, you are too late to come back to your home,
and you should not drive too fast on this road."*

When I look again where she last stood
the magnolia tree with its white blossoms
is swaying in the breeze.

Vine Rose

Is she drunk in the daytime?
Or her gyrations merely because of the vigorous spring breeze?
Prostrate, she can't seem to keep herself steady.

Until the flowers bud,
then she grows straight up looking at the sky.
Never even winking at the boys.

She lives, perhaps unwillingly
as if she were compelled by someone
to apply deep red rouge on her lips.
Touting admirers to come to her in the daytime.

Hiding her sharp thorns behind the green leaves,
she frequently crosses the neighboring yard.
It seems impossible to restrain her sexual desire.

Apple Memories

At Hillview Farm each fall
apples hang in clusters
on the branches appetizingly.

I pick the ripe red apples,
filling basket after basket.
My children looking on.

More than the red fruit in my hands
these apples are made up of blue skies, water and wind
and pleasing sunshine.

After awhile the cheeks of the apples
look like the glowing cheeks
of my smiling children—
laughing happily
gathering up the fruit
scooping them into baskets.

And the apples also
seem to be laughing.

Do the apples keep these memories for a long time, I wonder?

April

April's cold claws still remain in places
and the winds in the alley
still blow harshly.

On the sunny side of the street a cat yawns.
Grinning from ear to ear it stretches out its front paws.
His protruding tongue lengthens to bathe its body, even its tail.
The helpful breeze licks, smoothes down its fur.

The forsythia blooms its diminutive yellow petals.
A broody hen broods over her chicks
One curious hatchling tries to climb onto its mother's back
slips down again and again.

Tree boughs stretch their bodies.
Their branches saturated by the spring haze.
Breezes extend their height long into the sky.

Weeds' Rebellion

After frequently exchanging whispers among the magnolias,
the weeds attack fields and streams.
There seems to be no protection against them.

I have no choice but to let you turn out into the fields.
Despite the remembrance of the painful frostbit winter
that permeated through the morning glow.

Yesterday's roads cast off their skin
and stirring from sleep the withering branches wriggle,
rutting bamboo buds jump up from their roots.

Although we suffered last winter, we enjoy the sweetness of spring.
The fallen leaves here and there plaintively sing of the sorrowful days
but the moths will spawn on the fallen leaves
and the azaleas will open their eyes to look at green fields.

The aching remembrance of past seasons is not forgotten.
But the fragrance of the flowers tempt me to go out into the grass
and the tender smile of the southern breeze pulls at my hair.

Journey with No Definite Objective

In a rural park I sit on a sloped wooden bench,
make a pillow of my arm for my head,
gaze up at the distant sky, lost in thought.

There are nine hundred lambs and one thousand swans
walking at a leisurely pace in line across the sky.
A faint crescent moon hangs between them.

A shepherd in white clothes with a staff in his hand follows slowly.
Sometimes the staff pokes its head into the crescent
pulling it up toward the herd of lambs.

There is no traffic cop or expert to expedite these movements,
to make sure that everything flows harmoniously.

Two groups of white birds high in the sky turn round and round,
their feathers floating on wind that seems lighter than air.

All of them drift toward me—lambs, swans and birds.
Balanced buoyantly on a journey
with no definite objective.

Story of the Half Moon

In the garden my three-year-old son gestures toward the half moon.
"Where did the other half go?" "Why is it broken?" he asks me.

I remember now that he has seen a full moon only one time.
And I tell him that the other half of the moon is resting somewhere in heaven.

Now, when I look at the half moon, I imagine
the place she rests is somewhere I too could have a relaxing hiatus.

A place where I could restore my soul,
forgetting every inextricably bound thing of this world.

A Writing Class by the Railroad

Our classroom resembles a rural hut in the countryside.
In a renovated railroad station on the Hudson Valley.
The seasons seem to arrive earlier here.

At the writers' center students cultivate their creativity.
Exchanging opinions like farmers in this valley—
trading seeds, talking over the weather.
Their discussions continue until evening.

The sound of the railroad sparks their imagination.
The whistle so loud they cannot speak, but only look to each other.
Their hopes spreading out further, following the endless railroad.
Propelling them to fly upward toward blue skies, like the birds of this valley.

At the writing class on the Hudson River where the yachts anchor,
students primp their feathers like showy canvases to sail.
They are a step ahead of the seasons,
their enthusiasm leading the way.

Despite the noise of the train
the roses bloom beautifully
and the red apples are ripe on the trees.

A Place Where Clouds Are Flowing

On a grassy knoll by the Hudson River, I lie down with my head on my arms.
To the west many clouds are floating about
at the mercy of the wind.

An airplane is flying high through the clouds; my eyes follow it.
My yearning is wafted on the breeze
and chases the clouds.

I long to fly far off
where clouds go.

The clouds that seem to beckon with hands,
the clouds I wish to follow.
Hoping to visit a beatific place
like a childhood dream.

My imaginings take me to a land
over the continent, across the ocean.
To my beloved homeland
where I first fell in love.

So over the clouds
like a flower that blossoms
I send my love.

In a Blacksmith Shop

The dragon tattoos on the solid muscles of both forearms come alive
as the blacksmith shapes a sharp knife on the anvil.

With the might of his strong arms
he manages skillfully with one hand holding a tong,
the other a hammer, as steel yields.

At first when steel enters the blacksmith shop it is cold and stiff.
But on the anvil even stubborn and wild steel has no choice
but to succumb.

After getting red in the face,
from the heat of the flames and the thrust of the hammer,
the steel becomes a milder character.

At one time, both anvil and hammer were wild steel.
But now they are producing useful things
together with their master.

Summer High Noon

Abandoned asphalt streets in New York City—nobody walks.
I look out the window where the air shimmers with intense and stifling heat.
The pendulum of the cuckoo clock strikes two.
Everyone in the office slacks off.

A black cat awakens, pulls at his whiskers
opens its jaws in a teeth-baring yawn,
humps up its back,
then lies down with outstretched front paws.

The murderous heat comes roll by roll.
Descending like the grasshoppers that invade the streets.
Like a film of gossamer, heat winds around my arm.

Too hot, I don't know whether I breathe or not.
Vigorous heat attacks me thoroughly, through eyes, mouth, armpit and groin. Uncountable rolls of wrapping heat seal up whole cities.

Cigarette Butts

Scattered at random on the ground.
Each body crumpled with different forms.

Broken and cracked.
The numerous teeth marks
and lipstick stains remain

ugly on the bodies.
Marks on marks,
scars on scars.

Enduring the pain of constant biting.
Keeping all of the stories of hardship within,
their small bodies never forgetting.

Once the smokers' best friends,
They are now weltered and trampled
by pedestrians.

Cigarettes made dizzy by smoke from cherry lips,
fascinated with fragrances.
They gave fealty to their master.

Gone now.
Cast off!

They are quietly waiting
to decompose.
Perhaps strike up again.

At the Margaret Mitchell House in Atlanta

Under the calm light her framed picture kindly welcomes visitors.
A typewriter holds a paper with words captured on half a page.

Cannons from the Civil War faintly thunder from the old machine.
But those sounds are drowned out from time to time by a guide who recounts her life.

I meet Scarlet O'Hara in another hanging picture frame.
She welcomes me with a smile; seems to say that tomorrow is another day.

I nod gently to the portrait,
fighting the impulse to wind the spring that would awaken the old phonograph player.

The bed and sofa in the room hint of the leisure in her life.
The cooking pots, spoons, forks and knives reveal the kitchen customs of those days.

In the course of looking around at the past, I wander to the exit door,
and my mind abruptly returns to the present.

At a Shopping Mall

In New York City my wife and I go together to the shopping mall.
With all its enticements
it seems to be waiting for customers.

We are poor country people though.
Not familiar with malls.
So we step slowly through the stores.

We push our large cart and look
with our eyes opened wide…
hunting for a discount corner
to purchase goods with a big sale price.

My wife shows an interest in buying kitchen appliances—
white porcelain tea pots, pottery jars and stainless steel pans.
Items she always longed to have
in our kitchen at home in Korea.

But on this occasion I try to calm her earnest desires.
Telling her that we could buy
the more expensive items
next time.

Then my wife scolds me vehemently
about a next time that is coming continually
again and again
and never arrives.

Korea My Homeland

Korea! My native land!
Just hearing the name makes my heart flutter.

How long I have lived away from my native country!
Even though I can never forget it in my dreaming.

My homeland in the Far East
This pleasant country where my ancestors dwelled for thousands of years.

A free county defended from the invasions of foreign nations.
In the ruins of war bloomed the rose of freedom.

Where the sun first comes up on the continent.
Where there are four seasons.

In March the countryside feels the start of spring.
My rural home with its rocks and hills.

The peaches and apricots in full bloom.
The breezes blowing soft and fresh.

Though time and tides flow away,
spring, summer, autumn and winter will return there
again and again.

Are my childhood friends still living there, I wonder?
Even though I am far away from my home
this yearning makes me grow fonder.

Loving this land where cherished dreams are realized.
I would like to mount up to the sky like a huge white crane.
And see Korea again.

Flower Watch

I return to my home country of Korea—
Walk along the riverside where clovers grow
where Seunee and I played together as children.
We were poor, but happy.

Sometimes we squatted in the clover fields
searching for four-leaf clovers all day long
—believing it might bring us luck.
But it was not easy to find.

Sometimes we bet on who would discover the first clover; but Seunee always won.
Sometimes she asked me to sing to her or kiss her cheek.
Or make a watch from the clover flowers to adorn her wrist.

At first I didn't know how to create this thing.
But I soon realized that to make one watch
two flowers must be equally joined together.

Now I stand alone in the vast clover plains
in the dusk where flowers are in full bloom.
I call for Seunee loudly, but there is no answer.
Only a lonely echo.

The Sorrow

I'm at the window with the green tea she sent me.
I'm drinking the leisure hour of the afternoon
contained wholly in the tea
that has brewed little by little.

The sorrow spreads silently like a shadow
and drifts like a wind.
Appearing unexpectedly from time to time
though it never seems to stand in the way of the wide steps of life.

Now it comes together
with the fragrance of the tea.
Then ebbs from me.

Like a mass of dough in the hands of a baker.
Could I knead this sorrow till it is pliable?
Or like soft down on a thistle
it possible for it to blow away completely?

While I drink slowly
she is with me silently.
Spreads over the quiet surface of the cup with fragrance
and slips into my heart.

Faded Letter

While putting my desk in order
I stumbled across a faded letter.

It seemed I wrote it a long time ago,
But now I no longer understand the words.

Vestiges of adolescence hang in the sky;
as a young yellow-colored butterfly.

I had painted a rainbow-colored dream on paper
and was delighted with you.

But even now you are bringing me flowers.
A floral perfume
that emanates from the drawings.

Like a hieroglyphic letter from ancient people
this becomes a legendary story.

At the moment I put the letter into the drawer
I see a butterfly float aimlessly away
outside my window.

A Lucky Day

All through the morning, every day, an obscure saxophone player in New York City wanders from place to place, setting up stage in Times Square, the Port Authority Bus Terminal, Grand Central Terminal or the Empire State Building.

He places his worn-out hat (his only other possession) upturned, in front of his feet.
With closed eyes he performs his favorite songs:
Oh Happy Day and *Gypsy's Nostalgia.*

Immersed in the playing he forgets his hunger, sorrow and loneliness.
When he plays the saxophone, it doesn't matter who listens.
But a lucky day is to hear loud applause from the audience.

Pedestrian Crosswalk at Times Square

I'm waiting for the traffic light to change to green.
People swarm around me…
clamoring to cross the busy street
within the seven seconds mandated by a machine.

They walk with hurried steps—
students with their smartphones, heads down, watch their screens;
young couples hugging, slap and tickle each other;
a whistling young man pulling at his jeans;
a middle-aged woman clutches a purse in one hand and a fox terrier in another;
an elderly man, wearing large sunglasses hobbles slowly.
While a disabled girl in a wheelchair moves determinedly.

To get to the other side they must move forward quickly—
Going with the flow…moving forward….just forward…
No option for backward motion.
Everyone moving equally.
In this short duration of time, a mass of people,
each with their own style,
moving.

The Observation Deck of the Empire State Building

The outdoor viewing area is always crowded with visitors.
Tourists gazing through the telescope to the downtown below
or scanning the distant horizon.

Couples in their wedding attire,
pose for their picture,
a bride with a bouquet by the safety fence.

Fathers carry their children on their shoulders
to show them the view
far off into the streets.

One man stands vertically on his friend's shoulder
to see the world from a more high ranking position.

An acrobatic teenager stands upright atop his friend's head.
Stretching his arms he shouts loudly:
" I am the tallest man in the world."

Just at that moment a nearby seagull is startled by the sound
and flying away toward the blue sky
evacuates uncontrollably on the deck floor.

Times Square

A crowded Starbucks has no seats for its customers.
Outside I drink my coffee standing—
a temporary stage in Times Square filled with all kinds of people.

I observe tourists in the busy street: a large crowd jumbled together.
Storytellers, young folks snapping pictures,
an accordion player passing his hat for money,
a bride and bridegroom at their wedding ceremony.

From where I stand it looks like they are all leading incredibly busy lives,
hurrying in step to the building's neon advertisement
that also moves ceaselessly.

Perhaps these people feel as if they are traveling together,
as if they are bewitched
by the flashing pace of billboards.

Among them only the yellow cabs move lazily
through the scurrying crowd of fast walkers.

While Polishing Darkness

I left the golf trophy in the corner of the living room for a long time.
So that its color was changed to an ugly dark rust.
So that I thought about throwing it away several times.

But now I finally polish it—it had been awaiting me.
And by rubbing with a dust-cloth saturated with toothpaste
I release the lights that were strongly fastened by time and tide.

I pull the dim letters—bound with tarnish—out from the darkness.
When the letters on the trophy break out
they jump up at me—shouting with joy all together!

When I first brought it to the living room it was glittering and brightly shining.
But through my neglect and unconcern
its fatigued body was bruised by darkness.

Is there anything that doesn't change from the original in this world?
Because of my laziness I have confined the trophy's glorious shine to a dark prison.

I polish it again it with a dry cloth;
Now the trophy seems to spread its wings into the sunbeams of early autumn.
The sound of glorious light is getting stronger and stronger.

The Snail

After an evening of slight rain
a snail tries to move
in haste.

But slowly creeps
on the leaf
of a morning glory.

With tentacles for eyes
its pace
is slow,
intermittent
even…

This snail seems to think
before reaching its conclusion—
to move
from the old to the new.

North to south
forest floor to a peak of ocean
from fine to windy days.

Leaving a glimmer of itself,
marking a trail for others to follow.
A snail carries its universe within a spiral shaped shell—
with all its thoughts and necessities.

Spending its effort all alone
preoccupied with moving to the next place only.
Solving its problems slowly.

White Porcelain Vase

On a small table in the corner of a Buddhist altar
sits a white porcelain vase.
How long has it been there I wonder?

The moonlight flows together with a stream
in the black and white painting
Two carps meet where the gentle waves
approach the side of the frame.

The warm sunshine enters the room
through the windows covered with Oriental paper.
The sunshine brightens the room and the full moon in the painting.
From another room, a wooden gong sounded by a priest is heard
faintly.

The bell permeates the empty void
softly filling the room fully.
Pushes me to renounce my mundane agonies
and flow along with the stream in the painting
of the antique white porcelain vase.

After awhile the windows are opened slightly.
Outside the dried leaves are scattered on the ground
by the brisk wind.

Han-Jae Lee has studied poetry at Chung-Ang University and Korea University, and in the United States at the Almaden Community Center (San Jose); at library workshops in Santa Cruz and San Jose; and at the Hudson Valley Writers' Center workshops in New York. In 2005 his poem, "A High-rise Apartment," won a silver award in a national contest sponsored by The National Assembly of Korea and The Federation of Korean Cultural Center. His first book, *A High-Rise Apartment*, was published in Korea in 2008. He also co-published three poetry anthologies, and his poems have appeared in several Korean literary magazines. He has been writing poetry in English since 2004; and in 2013 his collection, *The Golden Gate Bridge and Other Natural Wonders* was published by River Sanctuary Publishing. His poem, "Cobweb," appeared in the *Catamaran Literary Reader*, Winter 2015 issue; "Flower Watch" and "The Sorrow," appeared in the *Monterey Poetry Review,* Fall 2016 issue. "Invisible Leash," appeared in the *CAESURA* 2017.

www.ingramcontent.com/pod-product-compliance
Lightning Source LLC
LaVergne TN
LVHW041510070426
835507LV00012B/1466